Alexa:

999 Tips and Tricks How to Use Your Personal Assistant to the Fullest

(Amazon Echo Show, Amazon Echo Look, Amazon Echo Dot and Amazon Echo)

Alexa Richardson

ISBN: 1976457874
ISBN-13: 978-1976457876

CONTENTS

Introduction   4

Chapter 1 – Your Personal Voice Assistant   6

Chapter 2 – Amazon Echo Look   16

Chapter 3 – The Echo Look & Your Privacy   21

Chapter 4 – Amazon Echo Style Check   24

Chapter 5 – The Echo Show   29

Chapter 6 –Voice Calls and the Drop in Function   38

Chapter 7 – How To Get Alexa To Play Movies And Videos   45

Chapter 8 – Alexa's Most Helpful Features   50

Chapter 9 – IFTTT   60

Chapter 10 – Skills   69

Chapter 11 – Helpful Tips   79

Conclusion   90

Thank you very much for getting this book!

I hope that you will really enjoy reading it. If you want to help me to produce more materials like this, then please leave a positive review on Amazon.

It really does make a difference!

Introduction

When Amazon launched its Echo device and the corresponding Alexa voice control system in 2014, it brought hands-free technology into the home of the general consumer. In the years since, Alexa has continued to be the most popular voice-activation software. It is expected to make up around 70% of the market in 2017, and is continuing to evolve with new offerings and features.

Alexa is an example of machine learning in action. It uses a smart artificial intelligence program to learn from the commands it's given, making it better and more useful the more you interact with it. This technology represents a drastic shift in how we as humans interact with machines. With the Skills API that lets anyone create their own commands for Alexa, it's also able to evolve at the whim of the market more effectively than any other smart technology.

When it comes to developments for Alexa, 2017 is an especially exciting year. Amazon released two new Alexa-enabled devices to their product line: The Echo Show and The Echo Look. Whereas past Echos only used microphones and speakers, these new products also have cameras, meaning Alexa can see you as well as hear you.

All of the Alexa-enabled devices are linked through an app that you can either download on your phone or view online (alexa.amazon.com). This is where you'll see a record of all the commands that you've given Alexa and can customize the settings of the device to suit your lifestyle. The app works best with

Amazon Fire tablets but can be accessed on any device.

If you've never experienced Alexa and want to get a sense of what using it is like, you can go to Echosim.io to scope it out without an Echo or other device. This page will let you test out voice commands and play around a bit with Alexa's capabilities, so you know whether buying a device is the right choice for you. Of course, now that you can get an Echo Dot for as cheap as $30, bringing Alexa into your home is an extremely affordable option.

The information in this book is designed to introduce you to all the ways Alexa can help you to manage your schedule and organize your life. For many users, she's the perfect personal assistant, always ready to answer your questions and carry out your commands.

The additions of the Look and Show to the Echo line make Alexa even more valuable. Using the camera on the Look, you can use the device as a personal stylist, helping you to organize your closet, plan your wardrobe, and choose the clothes that make you look your best; if this intrigues you, there's more information in chapters 3 and 4.

Amazon has also added a new feature to Alexa in anticipation of the release of the Show, Alexa Calling, which is its own version of a FaceTime or Skype application. This gives you hands-free calling to anyone who has installed the Alexa app, along with some features not included on similar applications, the details of which are explored in chapter 2.

Whether you're considering your first foray into the world of Alexa or just bought a new device and want to find out everything it has to offer, the information in this book will tell you everything you need to know about Alexa's capabilities as a personal assistant—and just how helpful she can be in your life.

Chapter 1 – Your Personal Voice Assistant

The voice control functionality of Alexa is extremely similar to using Siri on a smart phone. If you haven't used this kind of device before, it can be initially somewhat jarring, but it's extremely easy to learn the basics. Alexa is always on to respond to your queries and commands whenever you're in your home; the more you use the service, the more acquainted you'll become with what kinds of questions it can answer, as well as the array of helpful functions it can perform.

Alexa debuted on the Amazon Echo, a wireless cylindrical speaker that can also function as a smart home hub. Since the release of the Echo in 2014, they've added several new devices that can communicate with Alexa. The Amazon Echo Dot is a smaller, hockey puck-sized Echo designed for home use, while the Echo Tap is a portable version of the speaker. Amazon also included limited Alexa functionality on all their FireTV products. These items range in price from around $30 for the Dot to around $180 for the full-sized echo.

All of the previous devices were focused on the microphone and speaker combination, but in 2017 Amazon took Alexa into the video realm. The Echo Look includes a camera along with the same audio performance as the Echo. The Echo Show takes it one step further, with a 7" display and a front-facing camera, for the first time letting Alexa show you pictures and videos. These devices cost a bit more (between $200 and $250) but are still extremely affordable, considering their functionality.

Regardless of which device you purchase, the first-time set-up is easy, even if this is your first time utilizing smart devices. When you take it out of the box and turn it on, the device will walk you through the set-up process.

Once this is done, you'll almost be ready to use your new device—all that's left to do is install the companion app on your smart phone. This app is completely free and works with both iOS and Android devices. It is where you can change any of the settings of your device, and also lets you see the command history or link your Alexa account to other services you'd like to use it for.

When you go into your app, you'll see a list of all the devices you have that can use Alexa. Be mindful when you change the settings if you have more than one device. Some changes will affect all of your devices, while others will apply only to one device or type of devices. It's a good idea to spend some time exploring the setting menu so you can get a better idea of your device's functions and features.

If you have a relatively small living space, Alexa can hear and respond to you from anywhere in your home. For larger spaces, Amazon offers a Voice Remote for $30. This can be paired with any Alexa device by going into the "Settings" menu on your Alexa app. Once paired, you can use it to communicate with your device, even if you're out of its hearing range.

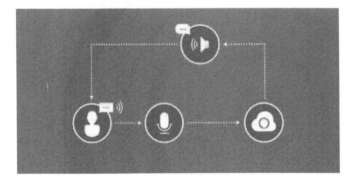

Voice recognition

Alexa is a pretty smart piece of software, and it's capable of hearing and processing user commands straight out of the box. The program learns your voice the more you use it, however, and when you're setting up a brand new device you might find it's helpful to go through the Voice Training program so there's no misunderstandings while you and Alexa are still getting to know each other.

You can find Voice Training in the Alexa app. Go to the Menu, and then choose Settings, where you should see the Voice Training option. It can be a somewhat lengthy process, so make sure you set aside at least a half-hour before you start. You'll say around 25 phrases out loud when prompted. This will help Alexa to work with your accent and speech patterns more easily in the future.

Giving commands

Alexa knows that you're talking to it when it hears the wake word. By default this is "Alexa," but there are other options available. You can switch the wake word in the settings section of the app. After you say the wake word, you can ask questions and make requests in natural language.

Will it rain tomorrow?

Play music by Bruno Mars

Add gelato to my shopping list

When is Thanksgiving?

Set an alarm for eight a.m.

What's the weather in Los Angeles this weekend?

There are a few commands you're likely to use frequently. At any point and in any skill you can say, "Alexa, stop," "Alexa, cancel," or "Alexa, help." This will interrupt whatever else is going on through your Echo. If you don't hear Alexa's response to a question, just say "Alexa, can you say that again?" and she'll repeat the last thing she said as many times as you need.

You don't have to be locked into a single phrasing or stilted way of speaking when you give commands to Alexa, one thing that makes it so much easier to use than many previous voice command products. If you want to change the volume, you can either say "turn it down" or "softer," and Alexa will understand you. You can alternatively give a numerical volume setting on a scale of 1-10, giving you lots of options. Not all commands will be as forgiving as this, but you won't have to do any linguistic contortions to make Alexa do what you want her to.

Location

Many of the most helpful features of Alexa—like giving you weather and traffic or ordering an Uber—can only be performed correctly if the device knows where you are. Because it's linked to your Amazon account, Alexa will already know your zip code, but you'll probably need to go into the Settings and manually enter your street address.

There's also the issue of a device's location within your home if you have multiple versions. Your device will be given a default name that's your first name followed by the product name (e.g. "Jill's Echo" or "Mark's FireStick") but this can get confusing if you have multiples of the same product. You can change the device's name under the Settings in the Alexa app. This way you'll know which one is in which room and be able to make changes accordingly.

Multiple users

Anyone who comes into your house can give Alexa orders just by saying her name, and you don't need to set up multiple user accounts to allow multiple people to use an Echo. If you want to be able to access the media libraries for multiple residents, however, you'll want to establish them as members of your household.

To do this, you have to go to your Amazon account page. Find the link that says "Household Profiles" and it will walk you through the process of adding someone to your household. You should have your house-mate with you when you do this, so they can enter any information the system needs when prompted. If you want to remove them later, you can do so at any time through this same page, though keep in mind they'll be unable to join another household for a period of six months.

Keep in mind that adding someone to your household affects more than the Echo's access to their library. It will also allow them to place orders through your Amazon account, give them access to some private areas of your account, and give their Amazon account many Prime benefits, if you're a member and they're not. Make sure whoever you're adding is someone you trust with your personal information.

Separate user accounts on an Echo are somewhat limited. You can't add items to the calendars or to-do lists of household users, for example, or order things through their account. The main value, as stated above, is that it allows music, audiobooks, and other files to be accessed from the household account through any connected Alexa device.

If you have roommates or children, you may want to limit their ability to place orders on your Amazon account when you're not there. The easiest way to do this is to create a passcode for voice purchases. You can do this in the Alexa app, under the Voice Purchasing menu. There's also an option here to turn off voice purchasing if you want to avoid the situation entirely.

Alerts and alarms

If you find your alarm is too quiet, you can change the volume in the Sounds & Notifications menu of the Settings on the Alexa app. You can also change the sound that plays for an alarm, choosing from a variety of ring options and even celebrity soundbites to wake you up in the morning.

The Sounds & Notifications menu is also where you'll be able to toggle audio confirmation. In the default setting, you'll know Alexa has heard the wake word or has finished receiving your command because the ring on the top of the speaker will light up. If you keep the Echo or other device in a place that's not easily seen, however, having it chime when it hears you can make sure you know when

Alexa is listening.

Music and other audio

The Amazon Echo was labeled as a wireless speaker when it was released, and although its Alexa capability makes it so much more than just a speaker, it also makes a fantastic voice-controlled and hands-free option for listening to your favorite songs, audiobooks, and podcasts.

The default music player on Alexa is Amazon Prime music. This gives you a relatively limited library, especially if you tend to listen to more esoteric music. If you have an account with iHeartRadio, Spotify, or Pandora, you can link these to your Alexa account and use them as your default player, instead.

Go to the Menu, then Settings, and under your Account choose Music & Media. Scroll down to "Customize my music service preferences" and pick "Choose default music services," where you can select Spotify or another service as your main music player. The only major music subscription services that aren't currently compatible with Alexa are Google Play and iTunes/Apple Music.

You can also use your Echo or other Alexa-equipped speaker as a regular Bluetooth speaker, having them play music from another device or drive in your home. You can set this up by putting the device in Bluetooth pairing mode. At this point, you can say "Alexa, pair" and the Echo speaker will pair with your device. When you're done, just say "Alexa, disconnect" and everything will resort to normal.

Alexa also offers direct integration with TuneIn, which is a service that gives you access to an array of live radio stations and a large podcast library. You can have Alexa bring up the latest episode of a podcast just by saying its name. The only downside to this service is that it will only bring up the most recent episode easily with voice command. You can get to prior episodes by saying "Play the previous episode," but would have to do this over and over until you reached the one you were looking for. If you want to listen to a specific past episode, your Echo can still play it, you'll just need to select it manually by searching for it in the Alexa app.

Finally, if you like listening to audiobooks, Alexa can read those to you, too. You can link your Audible account directly to your account and then say, "Alexa, read the audiobook" and say the title of the book. If you don't have an audible account, you can also have Alexa read you books from your Kindle library. She can even pick up at the same spot where you left off the last time you were reading. Keep in mind, though, that if you have Alexa read your Kindle books she'll do so in her robotic voice, which some people find distracting, and which is certainly no substitute for professional narration.

Chapter 2 – Amazon Echo Look

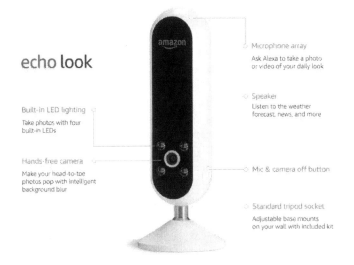

By now I'm sure you have seen the Amazon Echo Look and wondered what is it and what it can do for you. Well, for a mere 200 dollars Amazon gives you your own personal assistant and stylist. Not only are you able to take advantage of Alexa's core features, Amazon also gives you the capability to provide a 360 degree view of your outfits and your own personal critic.

Alexa as your Stylist

With this device, Alexa now becomes your stylist and her main purpose is to make you look amazing. This Alexa device is intended to be in your bedroom or near your closet – whatever works best for you.

With Echo Look, allows you to take full-length photos of your daily, weekly or even hourly looks by simply using your voice. The camera allows you to blur the background so that no one sees you surrounds and to enable your outfits to pop. In turn, it provides you with clean, share ready photos.

The echo Look also allows you to get a live view of your outfit with the Echo Look app. You can also use Alexa to take a short video so you can see yourself from every angle.

The camera and video functionality make it easier to get a full view of your outfit. The Echo Look's camera is enclosed by several small LED Lights which aim at providing you with a perfect, well-lit photo.

The camera is activated by simply using Alexa's wake word and adding the phrase "take a photo". When you say, "Alexa, take my photo", prepare to be captured. If you are looking to view your outfit in motion simply tell Alexa – "Alexa, take a video". After your image is taken the photos or videos are then uploaded to Amazon's cloud servers. The photos and videos are then sent to the associated smartphone application.

The Echo Look can be unpurposely aimed at the modern millennial. It is positioning itself as a fashion assistant. Once the Look takes a photo it will compare your outfits and make suggestions for various other fashion options.

You've finally gotten around to purchasing the Amazon Look, it's come in the mail and this is the moment you have been waiting for. You open the box and find the items listed below:

- The Amazon Echo Look device

  The Amazon Echo Look is Amazon's first device with a voice activated camera. The device is white with a black face with white buttons. The Echo Look mimics the shape of an oversized pill — it is a cylinder with rounded ends. It sits on a stand or mounts to a wall

  The device also comes with a *white base with a silver leg*. The device has the ability to sit atop a desk or it can be mounted with the included wall mounting kit. This kit includes wall plates, screws, anchors, and instructions. The device also comes with the following:

- Power Adapter with a 7.9-foot cable.
- Quick start guide
- Things to try card

The Amazon Echo Look can be directly compared to the Amazon Echo. Although it is shaped differently and the Amazon Echo lacks the use of a front-facing camera, the 2 devices are quite similar.

Portable	No	No
Power	Power adapter	Power adapter
Wi-Fi	802.11a/b/g/n Dual-band (2.4 GHz and 5 GHz)	802.11a/b/g/n Dual-band, dual antenna (MIMO. 2.4 GHz and 5 GHz)
Alexa Activation	Wake word Action button	Wake word
Camera	No	Yes
Buttons and Lights	Light Ring Action button Mute button	Front Light Ring Mic/Camera Off button Mic/Camera Off indicator
Bluetooth	Yes	No

Audio Input		
Bluetooth Audio Output	Yes	No
AUX Audio Input	No	No
AUX Audio Output	No	No
Compatible with Alexa Voice Remote	Yes	No
Accessories	Alexa Voice Remote*	Wall mount kit
Media Storage	No	Cloud
Alexa app	Yes	Yes
Echo Look app	No	Yes

Chapter 3 – The Echo Look & Your Privacy

With the advent of the Echo Look many people, rightfully so, have been concerned about the privacy of their video and face. The Echo Look essentially puts a camera in your bedroom. However, Amazon assures its users that their information is indeed safe. They do so by using the following security measures:

- Disallowing third-party application installation on the device
- Rigorous security reviews
- Encryption of images and communication between Echo Look, the Echo Look app, and Amazon servers.
- Amazon doesn't provide any personal information to advertisers or third-party sites that display Amazon's interest-based ads, according to the company.

If you still aren't completely sold on Amazon's security measures, there is a mute button on the side of the device which mutes the device and masks the camera. If that still isn't enough, unplug your device when it's not in use. Fortunately for you, your device remembers everything from the Amazon Alexa application and it will not hurt anything.

Ironically, everything that can be done with Amazon Look selfies, can already be done using the pictures that people have taken and posted online to a variety of social media sites. These pictures are not company specific and if warranted, anyone can get their hands on them. The only major difference between taking the cute selfies for Snapchat, Instagram and Facebook than with the Echo Look is that the Echo Look can give feedback on your "style" privately via the "Style Check" skill.

When you are seeking feedback on a specific outfit or photo this involves the image being backed up in the cloud, which can be done by Apple or Google and sending it out to social networks, messaging apps, text messaging or email.

Contrary to popular belief, taking pictures with a smartphone and sharing it online is still significantly insecure.

The Echo Look takes selfies to a new level, especially for beauty and fashion bloggers who now have the power to give their readers 360 outfit views. Not only are they able to get a full frontal and a 360 view – they are handsfree and can be taken simply with an Alexa command. The Look will draw in a large number of millennials looking to show their personal style to the world.

Chapter 4 – Amazon Echo Style Check

Style Check is a new skill which is specifically made for the Amazon Look. It keeps you looking your best by using machine learning algorithms and advice from a top fashion specialist in order to keep your look on point.

What do you have to do?

All you have to do in order to get the Echo Look to work her magic is submit 2 photos. Once your photos are submitted you will get an opinion on which outfits looks best on you based on the outfit's fit, color scheme, current popular trends and your body type. The more you interact with the system and provide your feedback, the smarter it will get. The more outfits you submit and the more the fashion specialist interact with you will also aid in making the Style Check skill more personalized to you.

Take the guessing out of your routine with this new skill. You no longer have to debate what to wear, this skill will do it for you. Style check will suggest an outfit that not only looks good on you but it will also suggest an outfit that fits with the weather.

The Echo Look provides the ability for users to get outfit recommendations for immediate use, a specific time frame, or even the next day. This feature allows you to plan your outfits in advance.

You also have the ability through Style Check to create a Look Book and even share your outfits with the world.

The Style Check team also wants to hear your feedback. If there is a feature you think could be beneficial or is needed just drop their support team an email at support@stylechecked.com.

How it works

In order to get started with your outfit submissions, all you need to do is provide StyleCheck with a location and time when prompted. StyleCheck will then suggest an outfit that fits the weather.

New features are constantly being added to make your fashion life easier. You already stress about enough things, what to wear shouldn't be one of them.

So, what can Style Check do your you?

Benefits:

- Reduce stress and stay appropriately dressed for all occasions

- No more guessing, second guessing and throwing clothes all over your room. Get some outfit certainty

- You will always be prepared for the weather. No more

boots in the heat or shorts in the rain.

Style Check Features:

- Receive outfit suggestions for instant use, a specific time frame, or even the next day so you can plan your outfit in advance
- Receive outfit suggestions for any location
- Fast and easy to use. Get outfit recommendations in less than 1 minute
- For the techie, here is how Style Check helps you. Outfit recommendations based on the following technology:
  - Uses Perez-Ineichen Solar Radiation models
  - ASHRAE based thermal comfort model techniques
  - Accurate Weather Data from http://Forecast.io
  - Uses CLO (clothing thermal Insulation) ratings

In order for the Echo Look to be able to accurately judge visual information or your outfit, it needs a way to collect the visual information. The camera simply collects image or the light which has bounced off an object and records it using a sensor. Once this is complete, the information is then rendered in binary code, which is the computers language of choice. Conversion to binary allows a computer to understand the information. The imagery is then assessed and judged.

Chapter 5 – The Echo Show

You might wonder just what the Echo Show can do. Well, you're about to find out, for this chapter will go over what the Echo Show is as a device, some of the cool things you can do with it, and some of the capabilities of the system.

About the Echo Show

The Echo Show is basically the Echo devices taken to the next level. This device will show you what you're looking for, and with the sound of your voice, you can control everything easily.

This system comes with a screen, a keyboard, and also some speakers in order to give you a crisp sound that is perfect for any room. It contains eight microphones noise cancellation, and even beam-forming technology. This system will react based on the commands even when music is playing.

In essence, this takes the Alexa system and enhances it completely. You can use this to call people, look up information, even read recipes to cook dinner. This device connects to Smart Home devices, and just from your voice alone, you control all of this.

Essentially, if you already have the Echo system, and you love it, you'll be able to take it a step further.

It's pretty light, being only about 41 ounces, about 7.4 inches high and 3.5 inches wide, so it's easy to carry around, and it even has dual-band Wi-Fi support. It all connects with the simple AC power chord that comes in there. The cable is about 6 feet long, so you can move it around.

It's quite an impressive system, and with Dolby stereo sound, it gives you the best that the Echo system has to offer, all in a simple package.

Why Would You Want This?

Are you someone that loves the Echo system? Then this is for you. With this system, it takes what the Echo had to offer, and gives you a screen.

If you loved your Echo device, but you don't like the idea of Alexa rattling off recipes in a confusing manner, or if you like visuals, this is perfect for you. The system comes with a screen, and you can connect to various sites to not only watch videos, but to look up information, find recipes, and you can even get an accurate look at the weather and the traffic report.

Plus, the Echo Show helps connect your Smart Home devices in a much easier manner. With the screen, you'll be able to look at the various aspects of your devices, allowing you to control them. This system does support various music services, allows you to call others, and you can use this to do so much more.

This is perfect of those on the g, who don't like to sit at the office and look up information. If you're fine with talking to Alexa, who will help you find various information, then this is for you.

Control Everything with Your voice

Probably the coolest part about this is that you can control everything with your voice. It allows you to have a hands-free system for calling. You can ask Alexa to do virtually anything.

With this, you can get videos and messages between not only the Alexa app and your Echo Show, but also other Echo devices. You can talk to people with the Echo system or your app, and it's just that simple.

Not only that, there is the Drop In function, which allows you to check in on other rooms. If you for example, put your kid to sleep and want to check in on them, rather than getting a baby monitor, you can have Alexa use Drop In to check that everything is all right.

With the voice feature, the future is now, and you can do all of this with the Alexa system.

The Echo Show is a great system that will allow you to expand your reach with these devices to new heights. You won't want to miss out on these features, and if you would like to control your entire home with just your voice, then this is the system for you.

Setting Up Your Echo Show

So, let's say you have the device, you're ready to get started with using this, but you don't know how to set it up. No worries, this chapter will take you step-by-step on how to set up your Echo Show so that you can use it in an efficient and rightful manner.

What Alexa Can Do

So, you've been hearing the name "Alexa" thrown around. What is it? What can it do? Well, you're about to find out.

Simply put, Alexa is a system that allows you to control your home and various devices with your voice. From music, to movies, to even asking what the weather and traffic will be, you can do all of this with the Alexa system. The Echo Show comes with a screen that shows you a picture, so that you can watch movies, play music, look up information, even use it to cook, and you can do all of this just with your voice.

Alexa is the system that you'll interact with when it comes to the Echo Show. We talked about what the Echo Show can do, but Alexa is really the one you'll be working with the most. It's a great voice control system, and you can even control your home via Smart Home devices. We'll go over that more later on, but for now, let's get to setting up this great system.

How to Set up The Echo Show System

So how do you set up the Echo Show system? Well, it's a lot easier than you might think. You probably think it involves some sort of tedious connection, but that isn't the case. It's actually just a few simple steps.

First, you need to grab your phone, download the Alexa app, and then sign in. You can get this for various web browsers and smartphones, and this is where you essentially manage the Echo Show and the other options that you need.

This is available for the following systems: FireOS 3.0 or higher, iOS 9.0 or higher, or Android 5.0 or higher. You need one of these three to connect to this.

Now, you can download the Alexa app from either the Amazon Appstore, the Apple Store, or Google Play depending on what mobile device you choose to use. If you want to, you can also check out http://alexa.amazon.com if you want to do this on a Safari, Firefox, Chrome, Edge, or Internet Explorer 10 or higher if you don't have any of those devices.

Your next step, once it's all downloaded, is to then power up the Echo Show. Now, what's cool about this is that you can simply plug this into any power outlet that you have, so if you want to move it around, you can. You can then follow the prompts that are there to set it up, such as choosing language, Wi-Fi connection, synching your Amazon account, and reviewing the terms and conditions. Once that's all set up, you'll be able to then start using it.

Now you can then sync up your contacts and accounts and add all of that fun stuff into there. But, if you want to sync up your voice to Alexa, you need to say the "wake word" which is essentially the word that'll wake the system up. You can then speak normally to Alexa. Typically, you have to say "Alexa" to begin the system but you can change the wake word, which we'll discuss further in the next section.

And that's it! That's all you need to do to set up your device. It's that simple, and you'll be able to start using this right away.

Talking to Alexa

Now, talking to your Alexa device is pretty interactive, but you need to say a certain word first. For the Echo Show, you must say the wake word, and then the request.

Now the problem with the word "Alexa" might be the fact that your name is Alexa, or maybe you've got a family member named Alexa. What do you do then? Well, that's pretty simple. To change this, you first need to choose a wake word from the following: Alexa, Amazon, Echo, Computer. Lots of people like to use Amazon or Echo instead of Alexa.

From there, to change this, you go to Settings, choose the device, go to Wake Word, and from there you select the word and then save.

If you want to change the wake word on the device directly instead of via the app, let's say if your phone needs charging, you go to Settings, then Device Options, then Wake Word, and then choose your word.

How to Personalize Your Device

There are a few personal steps that you can take to really make your device your own. These are ideally done now, so that you can use the device immediately.

Now, if you move for example, and the address saved in Alexa is your old address, you can change this. To do so, go to Settings, choose your device, choose the Device Location, and then Edit. Once you fix the address, you can then choose Save. You can do this either on the device itself, or on the Alexa app

Alexa also has a lot of skills. These skills can help not only connect your home devices, but also help you play games, check social media, or even tell you of upcoming events. How do you use this though? Well, it's that simple.

To do this, go to the app or say the word Skills. From there, you can then choose a specific skill, and once that's ready, you can open the page with the details, and then you can select the Enable Skill option. This is also how you connect third-party music and movie services such as Netflix, so keep that in mind.

You can even have Alexa put calendar events in. You can say "what's my next event" to find out what's next. You can say "add ___ to my calendar for (day) at (time)" in order to add events to this. If you already know of an event, you can say "add event to my calendar. If you need to delete an event, you can choose it manually, or say "delete my (time) event" and it'll be deleted.

Finally, you can add traffic info to your Echo Show to give you an idea of what your commute will be like. To enable this, go to Settings, then Accounts and choose Traffic, and from there, put in the starting and ending point, and then choose Save changes to save the changes that you need to.

When it's time to get the traffic update, you can say "how's traffic," "what's my commute," or "what's traffic like right now" in order to get a feel for what you'll be facing in terms of traffic. The same goes for weather once you put in the device location and saying, "what's the weather" or "show me the weather" and you'll get to see it. You can also ask if it'll rain/snow/be hot or cold if you so want to, and you can check the weather in various cities. That's that simple, but so very useful.

The Echo Show is an awesome device, and setup for it is pretty easy. Once you have it put together, you'll know what to do, and you'll be able to control your devices with your voice almost immediately.

Chapter 6 –Voice Calls and the Drop in Function

Now, the cool thing about the Echo Show is that not only can you call people, but you can also chat with them as well via voice. It is a means to almost replace video calls, and with Alexa, you can use it to almost control any sort of communication function. How do you use this though? Well, you're about to find out.

Setting up voice chats

Setting up voice chats is actually quite easy. To do so, you first need to download the Alexa app to your smartphone. From there, you can verify your mobile number and import the contacts to the Alexa app. Once Alexa has the contacts stored, you can then tell your friends about it if you desire, or just call them from the phone.

Now, to call someone, you need to sync your contacts to the app, and then say "Alexa, call ____" and it'll do that.

If someone decides to call you, there will be a green light on your Echo Show. If you want to answer it say "Alexa, answer" and if you don't, say "Alexa, ignore" and it'll do that.

Messaging with Alexa

If you want to message someone using the Alexa system, you can simply do so. This is a great function, because you just need to tell Alexa to do it, say what you want to say, and it'll then send it.

For example, if you need to text your dad, say "Alexa, message dad" and then say your message. It's that simple.

If you have messages, then it might be best to check them right away. You can do so with the Echo Show as well. To do this, you first need to receive a message. You'll see a yellow light followed by a chime whenever you have one. You'll also be notified on the app in case you're not home to check it.

If you want to check your messages, say "Alexa, play my messages," or "Alexa, play ___'s messages" if you want it to just play a couple of messages from a certain person.

The best part about this is that you can use this with other Echo systems, and even with devices that aren't Echo systems. You can still call and message others if you want with this device. If you want to use this with people that don't have an Echo, can you still call or message from there. To do that, you need to make sure that they have the app downloaded so that calling and messaging is enabled.

With this system, you typically will use the calling and messaging function for everyone, and only use the Drop In function for those that you're close to, and to other Echos to check in on them. We'll go over what Drop In is later on.

The best part about this is that calling and messaging is free. You don't have to pay anything, just make sure you have a phone service provider with a verified number, and other people have the Alexa app downloaded.

The best position for recognition

One of the biggest things you might be concerned about, is placement of the Echo Show when it comes to calling. You want Alexa to pick up the calls and let you hear them, but you might wonder where you should put it. Thankfully, you're about to find out.

The ideal location for your Echo Show when it comes to calling is in the same room that you're in. That's because it'll allow for the least amount of interference, and this is a great way to hands-free call without having to blow out the speakers and such on your mobile device. You can take your Echo Show with you if you do want to move it to another room.

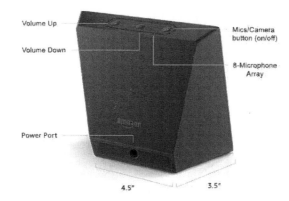

Volume Up

Volume Down

Mics/Camera
button (on/off)

8-Microphone
Array

Power Port

4.5"   3.5"

When it comes to the situation where you want to keep the Echo Show in one place, but you want to still call from multiple locations, it's ideal that you put it in a space with the least amount of interference from electronic devices, and from walls. You should also make sure that Alexa can hear you, and you can test this by asking her something. If she responds, then you'll be able to make calls or have her message people. It's really up to you where you put it.

Ideally, keeping it in the living room so that you have access to it from other locations can be your best option. You can always test it by having others call, or make calls or ask Alexa to do other functions as well.

It's also a good idea to put this in your office as well, especially if you spend a lot of time in there and have a lot of video calls. You can ask Alexa to dial various numbers, and you can even see the person on the other end. That's the beauty of the Echo Show in comparison to other Echo systems. You can see the person, and do many other things as well, right from the comfort of your own home.

Calling is super simple with this device, and this chapter showed you just how to get started with this.

The Echo Show also contains another interesting feature called Drop In. Drop In is an interesting system that can be used not only to check on others, but it's even an intercom system. How do you use it though? Well, you're about to find out.

The Intent of Drop-In

The Drop-In system is a new piggyback system that's used for voice calling. This is actually intended to be used to call friends and family set up on the same system to check in on them. However, if you have multiple Echos or Echo Dots around the home, it can even be used as an intercom system.

For example, if you're cooking dinner and the kids are upstairs, or your husband is in the office and the food is ready, you can Drop In from the kitchen to the upstairs or office Echo, simply by using the Alexa app on the phone. It's pretty wild.

This is a system that lets you literally Drop In wherever you want to. The other person doesn't have to answer, and it connects you automatically to work like an intercom system in the house. You can speak and hear anything happen to the intercom system that you have it connected to.

If you use this via the Echo Show, you'll see the contact on the window once you connect to them.

How to Use It

To use it, you first need at least one Echo, and one Alexa app that is installed and connected to the Echo. The Alexa app allows you to Drop In but you can't receive the call.

Now, to begin you need to make sure that you have the app up to date, and if you're not already subscribed to it, sign up for Alexa Calling and Messaging. Once that's done, open up the app, tap the conversations picture, which is basically the text bubble, follow the prompts, which is basically the caller information and number, and then it's all set up.

Now, you'll want to set it up to a specific speaker by pressing the Alexa app, tapping the hamburger picture, going to the settings function, and then choosing a speaker from the list. Make sure that when you go to the General setting, and make sure that it says On beneath the Drop In choice if you want calls from others. If you do want to restrict it, press Drop In and then touch Only My household.

To have Alexa Drop In on someone, you can simply say "Alexa, Drop In on ____" and the line being the contact name. You can manually do this by opening the app, going to Conversations, and from there choosing the conversation contact that allows you to Drop In and tap the Drop In that's located at the blue bar near the top.

You can also go to the Contacts tab in the right upper corner, press Drop In after choosing the contact, which is the icon beneath where their name is.

To use this as an intercom device, you first got to name the devices, you can then talk to Alexa and say, "Alexa Drop In on (room specified)" and then it'll Drop In on the room. You can manually do this too, but usually Alexa works better.

Enabling contacts to Drop In

Now, this can be an invasion of privacy on many fronts, but Amazon won't just let anyone Drop In. It has to be from the contacts that you allow to Drop In on you, and you must have Drop In enabled on them.

To set this up, first go to the Alexa app and press the tab called Conversations. Go to the contact icon, the one that looks like a person, and then choose a name from your contacts. You can then touch the toggle and choose Contact can Drop In anytime. You can then check your contacts by going to the menu and choosing yourself. Then, check under what's called Others Who Can Drop In on My Devices and make sure that everyone who has permission is listed. You can press Remove if you don't want someone dropping in on you.

If you want to stop Drop In, press Do Not Disturb.

The Drop In function is a neat little addition that allows you to communicate with other areas of the home. Obviously do consider the privacy aspect of this, and make sure it's not too invasive. However, it's still a pretty amazing system, and one that can be used to help make communication a whole lot simpler.

Chapter 7 – How To Get Alexa To Play Movies And Videos

With the Echo Show, it gives you a chance to use Alexa to connect to various movie and streaming services. You can play videos on your Echo Show. How do you do this though? Well, you're about to find out.

Linking Streaming Sites to Alexa

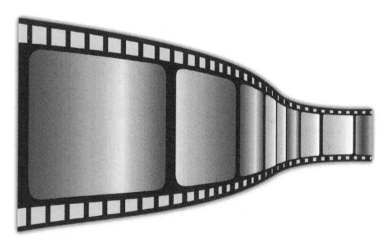

With Alexa, you'll need to link the streaming services to this. It's pretty simple, but it'll allow you to access Netflix and other services.

To begin, you should first link the service to Alexa. You'll need to initially open the Alexa app, choose the app that needs to be linked, add in the login information, or create a new one, and from there, follow the on-screen prompts in order to complete this.

Now, let's take Hulu for example. You can choose Hulu, add in your account details, and from there, Alexa will allow you to stream this.

To do so, you can have Alexa open up Netflix by saying "Alexa, open up Netflix" and it will. From there, you can choose the movie, or if you know what you want, say it to Alexa. Say "Alexa, play ____" and Alexa will play the video that you want to watch. Streaming has never been easier, and you'll be able to use this with Alexa and the Echo Show efficiently.

Choosing an Amazon Video on Echo Show

To watch an Amazon video, it's basically the same thing. Amazon video is a free service for those that have Amazon Prime, and you'll be able to watch any of the eligible shows on this. You should first make sure Alexa is connected to this through the Echo Show, and then from there, you'll be able to use the service.

Typically, you can do a voice search on everything, and Alexa will provide you with what you need. For example, if you want to look for a video from your library, or maybe something you've had on your watch list, you can say "show me the video library" or say, "show me the watch list." Alexa will give you a full list, and you can go from there.

If you have a title in mind, you can say to Alexa "Alexa, show me _____" for the title of the show. If you don't get a response, sometimes searching via the name of the TV series works. If you want to watch Game of Thrones for example, you say "Alexa, search for Game of Thrones" and it'll pop up.

Now, if you want to look for an actor or genre. Maybe you really want to watch that new Johnny Depp movie, but you can't remember the name of it, you can say "Alexa, show me Johnny Depp movies." And she'll do so. If you're just browsing online and you're looking in a certain genre, you can simply say "Alexa, show me (genre)" and she'll give you movies based in that genre.

You can even control what movie you want to say, and

season of a show, simply by saying "Watch ____" or "Watch (tv series name) season (number)" and you'll get Alexa to play that. You can tell it to skip ahead by saying "Alexa, go back (x seconds/minutes/hours)" and you can do the same by saying "Alexa skip ahead x (seconds/minutes/hours." Alexa can do all of this and so much more, and you can tell it as well to go to the next episode too.

Watching movies and shows is so simple with the Echo Show, for it will give you the information immediately just by talking to it.

Watching YouTube on the Echo Show

Another app that many like to watch is YouTube on the Echo Show. With this, you can ask it to play virtually any sort of video. For example, if you want to watch videos of puppies, say "Alexa, show my puppy videos on YouTube." You'll get a full list of the various puppy videos that are available, and once you choose one, you can say "play" "pause" and "rewind" when watching this. After you've chosen the selected video, the Echo Show will even give you other options if you want to watch more. So, in essence, you won't stop watching the dog videos unless you say to do so.

Now, if you want to play the search results, you can say "play dog videos on YouTube." From there, the Echo Show will find the first dog video, and then it'll continue to play them all the way through the queue, which is pretty awesome.

You can also use the voice control for playback options that are in the video. You can first tap the screen to find these options, and from there, use them whenever you're navigating through videos. Playing videos on YouTube has never been easier with the Echo Show, and pairing it with Alexa gives you a whole range of skills.

The Echo Show is a great way to play various movies and videos, and with the screen that it has, you'll be able to see the great content that you can watch easily, and control it all from your voice.

Chapter 8 – Alexa's Most Helpful Features

While previous Echo models don't have the camera and video features of the new Look and Show, they still come with a plethora of options that make them extremely handy as digital personal assistants. One of the broadest ways Alexa can be useful is as a hands-free way to access the wealth of information on the internet. Most questions you pose to Alexa will result in a concise verbal response, and as the program learns while you use it, she'll be able to give you ever more accurate responses to your queries.

The seven microphones on the Echo use a specialized beam technology to isolate your voice from the other sounds that might be going on in the house. Because of this it has an impressively wide range, likely wider than you might expect. Unless you have an especially large house, Alexa will be able to hear you from pretty much every room—probably even beyond the range where you can hear her response. The video and camera features of the Look and Show are the only ones that aren't unidirectional, and can't be used as effectively from multiple rooms at once.

But those screens, as was mentioned in their chapters, give

you a lot of benefits of their own. You can ask any Alexa device to check your schedule and tell you what's coming up on your calendar, or ask it to add a new event at a given time. With an Echo Show, you can see those events on your screen, making it much quicker and easier to track which upcoming days are your busiest, as opposed to having her read off every entry on the calendar.

Regardless of which device you have, linking Alexa to your Google Calendar is the most useful thing you can do to turn Alexa into your perfect digital personal assistant. You can do this by going to your Settings on the Alexa app, then going into Account and Calendar, where there's an easy option to link to Google.

The Alexa app is also where you can manage all of your shopping and to-do lists that you've asked Alexa to add items to. Again, the Show gives you some definite benefits for this skill, displaying your lists on the screen on command so you don't have to go into the app, but regardless of which device you have you can check your lists at any time through the app on your phone, or have Alexa read the items to you for a hands-free option.

As with calendar entries, you can link various other to-do list and shopping list apps to your account and use your Echo to control these apps with your voice. This can give you an expanded range of list options over the on-board ones Alexa generates already, helping you to stay organized and get to all of you various events and activities on time.

Alarms, lists, and keeping track of your events are the most common uses for Alexa across the board. If you're in the middle of something and can't look up at the clock, you can have her give you the time, or tell her to set an alarm for a certain time so you know when it's time to go to work or take care of other tasks.

There are also some tasks that are equally useful but less flashy and so don't get talked about as much when people are touting the benefits of Alexa. The fact that she can function as a hands-free calculator is one of these. If you're balancing your checkbook, asking Alexa to confirm your math can make sure you're coming up with the right figures from your calculations.

These math skills are perhaps at their most useful in the kitchen. Alexa can quickly perform measurement conversions. If your recipe lists things in grams and the packaging is in ounces, that used to mean putting everything down to take out your phone and search for the conversion, or else simply guessing and hoping it turned out right. With an Echo or other Alexa-enabled device, you can simply ask for the answer and you'll get it.

News briefings

If you ask Alexa "What's new?" she'll give you the run-down of the day's top headlines in a Flash Briefing. You can customize what news you get when you pose this question by going into the Settings on the Alexa app. Select Account, then Flash Briefing, and you'll see a wide array of sources that Alexa can reference when putting together your daily report.

"Alexa, play my video flash briefing."

Depending on your preferences, you can aim the news toward world events or focus on more local happenings. You can add in updates on the sports that you follow, get financial news, or even find out about the latest celebrity gossip. If the options that come with the app don't seem to have what you're looking for, there are plenty of Alexa skills that can supplement your options; check out the next chapter for more info on those.

Keep in mind that not all the news sources will come with audio. Alexa will read you the ones that are text-based, in her usual robotic tone, which some people find jarring. This is most likely to be a problem if you're asking her for updates on the stock market; her pronunciation of the symbols may be difficult to parse through.

Traffic

Once you've entered the street address for the compatible device (which you can do through the Settings on the app) Alexa will give you accurate and up to the minute accounts of current traffic conditions. You can also give her the address of your destination and she'll figure out the fastest route for you to take.

You can save time on that last step by storing the address of your most frequent destinations. Go to the app Settings, then Account, and finally Traffic. Enter your work address, for example, and you can simply ask, "Alexa, how long is the commute to work?" She'll tell you what to expect on your drive to the office.

Shopping

Alexa will automatically be linked to your Amazon account when you set it up, letting you order things through the site with voice commands. This option used to be limited to items you had previously purchased, but Amazon recently expanded the options to a whole host of Prime-eligible products.

There are limitations to what you can buy through Alexa. Currently, you can't use her to buy anything from the Pantry, or any Amazon Fresh or Amazon Now items. You also can't use Alexa to buy clothes, shoes, or jewelry. It's possible this limitation on fashion and accessories will lessen or go away entirely now that they've released the Look, but for now you'll still have to order your clothes on the actual site.

You can also use Alexa to order items from other companies, though it will take a bit more set-up. If the brand offers a Skill for Alexa, enabling it will let you link your account on that site to her voice order capabilities. Exactly what you can order will depend on the company and the Skill; check out the next chapter for more information on Skills.

Alexa and smart homes

It doesn't take a big budget to set up a smart home using Alexa. You can buy smart plugs for around $35-$40 that will plug in to any standard outlet, and can be used to power a wide range of devices. The smart plugs from WeMo and TP-Link work especially well with Alexa. You can use voice control to turn any device running through a smart plug on or off on command. This will let you use voice control on any light fixtures that plug into outlets without having to purchase smart bulbs.

Of course, if you want to set up a more elaborate smart home system, Alexa will still function beautifully as a hub. Alexa is compatible with a wide range of smart devices, including

Philips Hue bulbs, Nest Learning thermostats, and devices from Wink, SmartThings, and Insteon. You can even find many appliances that come equipped with smart technology, like the WeMo-enabled coffee maker. Which items you buy will depend on your lifestyle, your budget, and how elaborate you want to make your smart home system.

If you have multiple smart devices in your home, you can also put them into groups to more easily control them. This will allow you to turn all the lights in a given room on or off at once, for example; you could even set up a Skill for when you're away on vacation, turning the lights on or off occasionally so it looks like you're home.

Placement of your device

The question of where to put an Echo or an Echo Dot was not a particularly involved one. If you lived in an apartment or small home, you could put it anywhere and interact with Alexa equally well; even in a large home, you could buy a Voice Remote or portable Echo Tap and get the full range of her skills anywhere.

With the Look and Show, this question gets a bit more involved. With the Look, the most obvious choice of where to put it is your bedroom, since it's designed to work with the clothes in your closet. This might not make sense, however, if you want the Look to be your only Alexa device and your bedroom is on the second floor, or otherwise isolated, which would limit the value of Alexa's other skills in the rest of your house.

The display screen on the Show makes it the most difficult one to find a home for. The screen is designed to be viewed easily from seven feet away, meaning you can see it from across the room when you need to, but not necessarily from the next room over—especially if there are walls in the way. You'll be able to use the voice command functions of Alexa in any room, so your main consideration should be where the screen will prove the most helpful.

While you might be tempted to put your Echo Show in a living room or office because those are the places you spend the most time, you may instead want to put it in your kitchen. You're likely to be in this room a lot while you're getting ready in the morning, which means it's the perfect place for quickfire questions about the weather or traffic, and the screen can show you what everyone in the household has on their agenda for the day.

Alexa can also be a great help at dinner time, displaying

recipes, checking cooking times, or setting timers that you can watch count down on the screen. The kitchen is also the room where you're least likely to already have a screen for watching videos or looking at images (although more and more fridges are coming with this option).

You can also easily manage multiple Alexa-compatible devices on the app, and with the variety of types of device that are soon to be available, getting more than one makes more sense than it did in the era of just the Echo. You could have a Show in the kitchen, a Look in your bedroom, a Dot for the office, and a Tap on-hand for taking out into the backyard—or whatever combination makes sense for your living space.

Chapter 9 – IFTTT

The acronym "IFTTT" stands for "If this, then that," and is a similar concept to the Alexa skills mentioned above. Like skills, IFTTT commands allow you to do more and control more devices with simple voice commands. Also like Skills, they're open for anyone to create.

Where IFTTT differs from the skills you can enable is in their ease of set-up. Whereas you have to be comfortable using the developer platform and doing some programming to create a skill, creating an IFTTT command is as easy as going to the website and following the simple onscreen prompts. Even home users with absolutely no experience with programming will be able to navigate these commands easily. Of course, you don't have to create your own commands if you don't want to. Just like with the skills, you can find a plethora of useful IFTTT recipes, known as applets, online for a variety of functions.

IFTTT is an online platform that allows you to easily connect and control devices and apps more intelligently. It is essentially a means of translating messages between devices so that you can allow one action (the "if then") to lead to another (the "then that") in a chain reaction. You can set up some fairly long and complex chains of commands using this platform, allowing you to greatly simplify the commands you say to Alexa to achieve a variety of tasks.

IFTTT
Put the internet to work for you.

When you use them correctly, IFTTT applets are arguably the easiest way to completely customize your Alexa interactions, without having to wait for another user or a developer to create the action that you need. You can also tweak the applets available pre-made online, which can be a great way to grow accustomed to the process when you're just getting started.

There are a few limitations on the IFTTT system. First of all, it is currently only supported by devices in the United States or United Kingdom; if you live in another country, you'll have to stick to skills. You can also only use IFTTT with devices and services that have set up a channel on the platform. Anyone with a product or service can inquire about creating a channel at any time, and the number of available channels is constantly growing—there were around 100 in July of 2014, but that number had grown to over 350 by the summer of 2017. Many of these channels come automatically pre-loaded with an array of applets specifically designed for

Alexa to get you started.

There are a few smart home kits and products that don't have an IFTTT channel. If you want to be able to use these commands, search the IFTTT channel list before you purchase a new smart product to make sure it's supported. There are some surprising services that can be used in IFTTT recipes, as well, including online platforms like Twitter and Instagram, along with personal devices like Fitbit.

You can loosely divide the channels available into three categories: online services (like Gmail or bitly), hardware and devices (Google Glass or smart appliances), and functions (like weather or date functions). These channels can be connected into the same daisy-chain recipes; for example, you can use a date or time trigger to power given devices on and off as well as send a notification to an online service.

While the concept behind IFTTT is simple, getting set up can be a bit trickier and time-consuming. You'll often have to download an app associated with the service if you haven't already in addition to enabling the channel. You also may need to create an account through the product or service's page. While all IFTTT channels are free to activate, some will only work if you've purchased the associated item or subscribed to a given service.

The more channels are added to IFTTT, the more useful the service gets. It can be used to make Alexa do all kinds of fun things. You can have it start your coffee brewing when a trigger from your fitbit tells Alexa you've woken up, for example, or have it turn your lights on and off at certain times while you're on vacation so it looks like someone's home. Once you have the basics of making recipes down and have the right channels, your possibilities are almost endless.

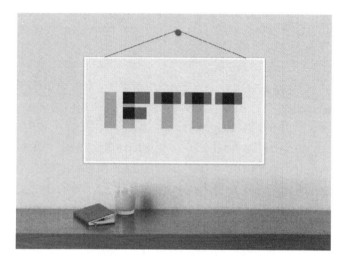

IFTTT recipes

There are three components to any IFTTT recipe: triggers, actions, and ingredients. The best way to differentiate them from each other is to use an example. Say you want your Christmas lights to turn on at sunset every night. The trigger in this example is the time that sunset occurs; the action is powering on; and the ingredients are the smart plugs your strands of lights are plugged into.

The way to chain applets together is to have the action of the first serve as the trigger of the second. You can do this as many times as you want. You can also tweak applets easily. If you decided you instead wanted the Christmas lights to come on when you said "Alexa, happy holidays," you could change the trigger to a voice command; the action and ingredients remain unaffected.

Every recipe starts with the phrase "ifthisthenthat" and builds from there. The online interface is very intuitive, walking you through each of the seven steps. If you mess up at any point along the way, you don't have to start over; just hit the back button until you get to the step you need to change.

The only limitation to the components you can use in the IFTTT are what kinds of things are available on the channel of the product or service you want to incorporate. Spend some time getting to know new channels as you enable them. Newer ones especially may be taking a gradual approach, which could mean that there aren't many actions available right now but there will be more in the future. Other services have certain limitations built-in, especially social media sites, which may seem silly to individual users but exist to prevent IFTTT from being used for spam.

Useful channels and applets

There are far too many channels to list all of them here, and with how often new ones are added, it would be outdated pretty quickly. Just like with skills, some of them will be fairly specialized or limited in their functionality, while others are must-haves for anyone with access to Alexa.

If you own any kind of smart device, you won't get the full

value out of it unless you also enable its corresponding channel on IFTTT. Products that have an especially useful channel include Philips Hue bulbs and Nest devices, like their thermostat or Protect smoke alarm. If you want to use IFTTT with your home entertainment system, Harmony brand remotes allow you to stack your TV, audio equipment, and gaming console in a single device that has an impressive IFTTT channel.

There are some neat devices that are mostly useful as an extension for IFTTT applets. One example of this is the Parrot Flower Power, a small device that you can insert into a flower pot or garden that will monitor the moisture and fertilizer content of the soil, as well as tracking the temperature and light levels. It's even smart enough to identify what kind of plant you have and what it needs to thrive. When the plant needs attention, you'll get an alert on your smart phone. If you've always wanted to have growing things in your home but have a historically black thumb, this just might be the perfect recipe for you.

Thanks to the ability to chain applets easily, you can create recipes that control all of the smart devices in your home with one simple phrase. One popular applet is "good night," which essentially gives your house a bedtime mode. Say that one phrase and you can have Alexa turn out the lights, turn off the TV, and adjust the temperature so it's ideal for sleeping.

Some of the coolest applets for the Philips Hue use the color options and dimming ability to excellent effect. You can have the lights brighten gradually when you wake up in the morning, giving you the effect of a natural sunrise and making the transition out of sleep less jarring. There's even an applet that makes the lights glow different colors depending on the weather outside, so there's no more wondering what to expect when you open your front door.

Some channels will give you unexpected side benefits. One example are WeMo smart plugs—another must-have channel for a smart home. By enabling it, you can not only use the plugs as ingredients in your recipes, but can also use it to track energy usage so you can identify devices that are huge drains on your power. You can then set up an applet to automatically turn off appliances left running in the background, saving you money on your electricity bills.

The Nest Protect smoke detector is another smart device with an excellent IFTTT channel that every home owner should check out if they haven't already done so. The applets provided on the channel can help you keep your home and family safe. You can get an alert when the battery needs replaced so you'll always know it's functioning correctly. It will also sense high levels of carbon monoxide and alert you if it's detected, then keep track of these instances so you can look for trends and prevent bigger problems.

Don't let this give you the assumption that IFTTT is only useful if you want to connect outside devices. It has a number of uses even if the only smart device in your home is an Echo. You can have it make your playlists into a Google Spreadsheet, for example, so easily keep track of which ones contain which songs, or share the info with people coming to a party so they can make requests.

Since you can use things like the weather, a date, or a time as the trigger, IFTTT is a great way to have Alexa tell you things without having to ask. Have it alert you when there's rain in the forecast so you don't forget your umbrella, or have it remind you of important dates like birthdays and anniversaries a few days ahead of time so they don't catch you by surprise.

Many online services also have very useful applets on their channel. If you're a sports fan, enabling the ESPN IFTTT channel will make it easier to keep track of your teams. You can set it up to automatically add their games to your calendar, and then send the final score to your phone once it's finished.

There are also many useful channels and applets that work with your phone. The applet "find my phone" is one of the simplest and most popular. Just tell Alexa "find my phone" and she'll make it ring. If you have old iPhones laying around, you can use applets with those, as well. The Manything channel lets you turn them into closed circuit cameras. Just mount the phone or set it up on a stand and make sure it's on the same WiFi network as Alexa. Manything will use the camera to record video footage which you can then access remotely, checking on the daily report or reviewing footage from the last month.

Alexa does lists especially well. When it's time to take your shopping list with you to the store, you can search for it on the Alexa app, but for a lot of people accessing their e-mail is easier. There's a pre-made applet on the IFTTT site that will send your shopping list to your inbox on command. Just turn the applet on and give IFTTT access to your e-mail service. You'll be able to enter up to five e-mail addresses, so everyone in the household can have access to the info.

Chapter 10 – Skills

Alexa's AI is designed to learn and change over time, and the arrays of Skills you can add to its arsenal are one way that you can control and customize how it learns. Skills expand the abilities of your Echo beyond even its impressive functions right out of the box; giving you more commands to interact with more services—and even letting you create your own, if you're adventurous enough.

You can think of a Skill as an app for Alexa. Like an app, they can be developed by anyone, and must be manually added to your device before you can use them. There is a store you can access through the Alexa app on your phone where you can browse the available skills, similar to an app store. There are currently over 12,000 skills to choose from, and that number continues to grow. Thankfully, you can limit your search by category to help you find the skills you're looking for, or look up a specific skill by name.

Activating a skill is incredibly easy. Once you know the name of the skill you want to use, simply say "Alexa, enable" followed by the skill's name. You'll be able to use it instantly, with no delay for downloading or installation.

Once installed, the skill will have an invocation that lets you use it. This is similar to the wake word that activates Alexa. It directs Alexa to the right skill to carry out your task, and can be the name of the company, the name of the skill, or some other easy to remember cue. As you activate more skills, you may find it helpful to keep a written record of each skill and its invocation, just in case you forget.

Because anyone can design a skill, some of them are more useful than others. Many are very specialized to work with a specific appliance or service; others are simply lacking in their functionality, or have issues that prevent them from working properly. If you're searching the skills on your own, you'll have to sift through a lot of options before you find the ones that will be useful for you.

To save you some trouble as you start looking through Alexa's skills, some of the most consistently useful ones have been identified here. They're divided into groups depending on their purpose. Certainly they're not the only useful skills available for Alexa, but they'll give you a good starting point and an idea of what kinds of skills you'll find on offer.

Around the home

There are loads of skills you'll find you use every day to help you organize your life. Alexa comes with the ability to make to-do lists and add items to your calendar, and there are many skills that enhance these features. Quick Events makes it easier to set reminders and add events to your calendar.

If you're an iPhone user, you can sends to-do list items you make with Alexa straight to your iPhone thanks to an applet made using the "If This, Then That" service. This is the same platform where you can set up your own command chains and sequences, and is a useful one to get familiar with if you own a lot of devices that are smart-compatible but don't automatically hook up to Alexa.

Skills can also be used to further customize your daily news flash. The NPR Hourly News Summary skill gives you a 5-minute briefing on the day's headlines, updated every hour so you know you're always on top of current events. There are similar skills available from the Associated Press, as well as other major news outlets like CNN and BBC.

When it comes to getting financial news, Alexa skills in the past have fallen short, mostly because of problems with pronunciation of the various stock symbols. One that avoids this problem is Opening Bell, which lets you say the natural name of the company rather than its symbol, making it easier to get the information you need.

Alexa skills can also be helpful in case of emergency—both digital and physical. If there's a data breach on a site you frequent, you can check to see if your account's been compromised using the "Have I Been Pwned?" skill. It can be somewhat tedious in the execution since you'll have to spell out your entire username, but it will quickly bring up any security breaches connected to your name.

If you fall or have another emergency in your home that makes you unable to reach your phone, Alexa can come to your aid. Ask My Buddy is a skill that will send a notification to a pre-selected emergency contact by text, SMS, or phone call to let them know you're in trouble. It's no substitute for 911, but it could save your life if you're in a bind.

You can call on Alexa for more minor emergencies, as well—like, say, losing your phone. The TrackR skill can help you find it. You have to install the corresponding app on your phone first. Once you do that, enable the skill and you can ask Alexa to find the phone and give you the address. If it's nearby, you can have Alexa make the phone play a loud ringtone, even when it's on silent, helping you find it quickly.

Going out

Communication used to be one of the few areas that your Echo couldn't help you with. The Alexa Calling feature on the app and Show has changed that, but while that lets you make calls, it still doesn't send text messages. For that, you'll need the Molly skill, which lets you set up voice-controlled SMS in a few easy steps.

Start by registering at SMSWithMolly.com. Once you do that

you can enable the skill and upload your contacts, giving them their own unique names. You can dictate your text to Alexa and she'll send it to the contact you designate—perfect for telling your friend you'll be a little late without interrupting your getting-ready routine.

If you're looking for a place nearby to go for dinner or drinks, you can enable the Yelp! Skill which can give you not only the names of local options but also their hours and phone number. You'll want to verify your address is entered correctly for the best results; you can do this in the Settings menu of your app.

The popular ride sharing sites Lyft and Uber have skills for Alexa, as well. Once enabled, you can have Alexa order you a ride, check on how long it's going to take to arrive, or even cancel it if you change your mind and decide you'd rather stay in.

Finally, if your social call is of a romantic nature, you may want to consider adding the 1-800-Flowers skill to your device. You'll also need to have an account with the site to use it. Once your account's linked, you can use a voice command to order flowers and have them delivered to any address.

Entertaining

Alexa's on-board features already make it a great benefit in the kitchen, whether that's setting a timer or alarm to tell you when the cookies are done baking or asking it for measurement conversions and potential substitutes during the course of preparing the recipe. With the addition of a few skills, though, Alexa can become an entertaining powerhouse, guaranteed to make your next dinner party or friendly gathering a roaring success.

When it comes to cooking, there are arrays of recipe apps that you can enable that will help you find and prepare delicious meals. Best Recipes gives you the option to look up recipes based on up to three ingredients then has the option of narrowing the results depending on what meal you're preparing. The Campbell's Kitchen skill gives you give new recipe options every day that you can have sent to the Alexa app so you can prepare them. There are also apps from AllRecipes and several celebrity chefs. If you have an Amazon Show, these functions become even more useful, since you'll be able to display the recipe right on the screen.

Many appliances will also come with Alexa skills that let you use voice control. A lot of the current appliances that offer this ability are on the higher end of the price scale and are somewhat specialized and gourmet in nature, like the Joule sous vie machine or the Anova Precision Cooker. The number of appliances that offer this kind of voice control connectivity is likely to expand in the future, however, and if an appliance is set up for smart control and Bluetooth or WiFi compatible, you can easily create your own skill to control it using the Alexa API.

If you'd rather order food than prepare it yourself, there are skills for that, too. Both Domino's and Pizza Hut offer skills that let you use voice activation to order your pizza. Other restaurants that offer delivery as an option are bound to follow suit as Alexa's popularity continues to grow.

Of course, a good party isn't just about what you eat—it's also about what you drink with it. There are a few apps to help you with this. MySomm is a skill that will help you to pair wine with food. It has hundreds of recommendations of what wines pair well with a range of ingredients. If you'd rather go the beer route, Check out the "What beer?" app, which will give you the same information but for beer instead of wine.

If your guests are more of the mixed drink crowd, check out the skill The Bartender. It has a library of over 12,000 cocktail recipes that it can recite to you on command. This speech-based answer can be a bit much to hear all at once if you're still learning how to make the drinks in question. The screen on the Show might help this out a bit, but in the meantime it's a great way to refresh on the ingredients or order of a drink you're not quite sure how to make correctly.

Music is another key aspect of any party. The Echo's incredible voice command capabilities when it comes to playing music have already been discussed earlier in the book, but you can also find an array of skills that can interact with a broader range of music subscription services, as well as helping you to set up customized playlists and other helpful entertainment features.

Skills for travel

While you might think about Alexa more for its applications in your home, there are some skills you can get for it that make it helpful for planning travel, too. Perhaps the most useful skill is the one for the travel site Kayak. You can't use voice command to book a trip, but you can use Alexa to help you look up the lowest fare prices so you can get the best price when you are ready to buy your tickets.

There are also some helpful skills related to the airport. If you have people coming in from out of town, you can use the Landing Times skill to find out whether a given flight is on time or delayed. It can track flights from all the major airlines, including American, Delta, United, Southwest, Air Canada, Alaska, Frontier, and Spirit.

If you're the one taking the trip, using the Airport Security Line Wait Times skill can tell you what kind of delays you should expect in the security line. It gives you real-time data from over 450 airports around the United States and can help you make sure you show up with enough time to make your flight.

Chapter 11 – Helpful Tips

It can be tricky to use Alexa to her fullest extent when you're first getting used to how she works. How to phrase your commands to get the results you're looking for is the biggest hurdle for most new users. Compared to previous voice control systems, she understands natural speaking patterns extremely well, but she can have a bit of trouble with certain voices or accents.

If you're getting a lot of frustrating "fail" messages, your first step should be to go through the voice training described in chapter 1. This will make sure that the problem isn't Alexa's ability to understand what you're saying.

If that still doesn't seem to fix the problem, you may need to investigate just which commands she recognizes. The website CNET has a list of every single Alexa command available and updates it regularly to accommodate changes to the software. If you want to see commands specific to a device or service, you can also find those easily with a quick online search. Take some time when you add a new device, skill, or IFTTT applet to research the associated commands. You may find this also clues you in to functions you didn't realize it had.

If you're having trouble with a skill, make sure you're using the right invocation. Because skills are created by outside users or companies, they are not always as intuitive as the functions that come with Alexa. Similarly, if you're using an applet, make sure you've got the right trigger, and that what you're trying to accomplish is actually supported by the channel.

Alexa constantly learns from the commands you give her, but if you want to speed up the process you can also guide her along by providing feedback. A card will pop up in the Echo app every time you ask Alexa a question or tell her to do something. You can use this to tell Amazon whether or not Alexa heard you right, information that will then be used to help her hear you better the next time.

One general piece of advice if you're trying to deepen your knowledge of Alexa's capabilities is to think beyond the obvious uses of some of the most common functions. Many people don't know that you can ask Alexa for the time in other regions of the world than where you're living. If your friend is visiting Australia and you want to know if it's a good time there to call and chat, just ask Alexa; if the city is over the dateline, she'll tell you the date as well.

Alexa is also knowledgeable about upcoming holidays. Being able to quickly find out what day of the week Christmas falls on can help you to plan out your vacation time. You can also ask Alexa to tell you exactly how many days you have left to shop, or how many days there are between any two dates that you give her.

Once you've activated IFTTT channels and enabled skills connected to certain services and devices, you can also use Alexa's variety of voice commands within these, as well. Asking "Where's my stuff?" will not only let you check on the status of any orders you've made through Amazon, it will also let you ask about the status of a pizza you ordered from Domino's, or tell you how far away your Uber is.

Even if you've had your Echo for a while, there might be things you didn't realize it could do or haven't had a chance yet to explore. The tips that follow in this chapter cover a range of topics to help flesh out your knowledge of Alexa.

The more you know about what she can do, the better you'll be able to use her to organize and simplify your life.

Software updates

Alexa exists in the cloud, which means it is always connected to the network and can be automatically updated on a continuing basis. Most of the time this happens seamlessly, but if your Wi-Fi network is spotty or otherwise temporarily interrupted you could miss an update from time to time.

If you hear of a new feature that's been released but it doesn't seem to be available on your device, you don't have to wait for the device to update again on its own. Forcing an update is easy. When you put your Echo on "Mute" so that it can't hear commands, it eventually gets bored and looks for ways to keep itself busy. This will include double checking for new updates and installing them if it finds any. This takes about 30 minutes to kick in, so it's best to do it when you won't need to use Alexa for a while, like while you're at work or when you're sleeping.

Naming functions

Earlier in the book we discussed how you can change the name of your device to make it easier to identify, an especially good idea if you have more than one Echo in your home. But you can also set names for many popular functions on Alexa. This can be helpful if you want to use them to do multiple things at once.

The timer is one example of this. You can assign each timer with a specific title, like "rice cooker" or "chicken." This lets you check on the status of a specific timer or cancel one timer while leaving the others going. If you want to see the status of all your timers at once, you can do so from within the Alexa app. You can do the same thing with your alarms, too.

You can also create names for other smart devices in your home, or create "profiles" that include multiple devices under one title. This is especially useful for setting up IFTTT applets. You can set up a profile group for every switch and light in the living room, for example, letting you turn them on or off with one command. There's no limit to how many devices can be in one group, or to how many profile groups you have.

Getting privacy

Most of the concerns people have about Alexa and her associated devices have to do with exactly what the service keeps track of. Though she's always listening, she doesn't actively kick on and start recording what you say until you say the right wake word. The "always listening" part of that is both what makes her so incredibly useful and what makes some people uncomfortable.

If you want to make sure that Alexa isn't eavesdropping on your more personal moments, you can easily mute any Echo device. All of them come equipped with a "Mute" button that completely disables the microphone. You'll know it's been muted successfully because the ring around the top of the Echo will turn red.

As was mentioned earlier, the cameras on the new Look and Show take the question of privacy and security to a new level. Both devices have a mute button just like the original Echo; pressing this button disables the camera along with the microphone. Unlike the microphones, the camera is unidirectional, which also means you can turn the device around or lay it down flat if it still bothers you to have the camera pointed your direction. If you have Alexa Calling, don't forget to put it in "Do Not Disturb" mode so none of your friends drop in on you unexpectedly.

Uploading music

There are a few different ways you can have Alexa play music that you own. If you've purchased it from Amazon, you can access it automatically through the player. You can also use the Bluetooth or Wi-Fi connection to stream music files stored on solid state drives in your home.

The Echo and associated devices don't come with any solid state memory, but you can upload your personal sound files directly to the Cloud. Just go to the Amazon Cloud Player site and you'll be able to upload and store up to 250 songs for free. This will let you tell Alexa to play them even through the app, letting you take your favorite songs everywhere without having to suck up the memory on your phone.

More music tips

designed by freepik.com

Sometimes you'll hear a snippet of song and get it stuck in your head. It can be infuriating trying to figure it out. This is a problem no more thanks to Alexa. You can ask her "Alexa, play the song that goes..." and sing the portion of the lyrics that you can remember. She's usually pretty good at getting a match, even if you don't know many of the lyrics.

If you just ask Alexa to play a song, she'll use whatever music service you have set as your default to do so. If you'd rather go through a different service, you'll have to specify this by including the phrase "on Spotify" (or whatever service you want to access) during your command.

If you want to keep a record of the songs you've played on the Echo, you can enable an applet through the IFTTT interface to do so. It will keep track of your play history and save it to a spreadsheet that you can review later. To go the other way and play a pre-made playlist on your Echo, you'll have to say a fairly specific command. Make sure you say the word "playlist" after you've said the name of the playlist; if it's not on your default music player, make sure you also tell her which service to find it on.

Decision making aids

Getting a piece of software to generate a random number is a fairly basic programming exercise, so it's not surprising that Alexa can do it so much as it's not a tool most people would think about. If you want to choose the team leader in a game of Trivial Pursuit or determine who get to pick the pizza toppings, you could have everyone guess a number and announce the closest to Alexa the winner.

If the choice you're trying to make only has two options, you can ask Alexa to flip a coin; she can also roll a set of dice. There's even an applet that will let you use Alexa as a magic 8-ball, though you should probably refrain from shaking and flipping your Echo.

Easter eggs and games

The people who developed Alexa have a sense of humor, and they've worked a lot of fun Easter eggs into the program. If you're not familiar with this term, it refers to a hidden feature placed into a piece of software for the user to "discover." For many people, a lot of the fun with Easter eggs comes from stumbling on them by accident, but if you're not concerned about spoilers, you can find extensive lists of them online. Most of them are related to the geek community or well-known pop culture touchstones if you're trying to find them for yourself.

There are other ways Alexa can help you pass the time. She'll play word games with you; Word Master is a particularly fun one. There are also a slew of different quizzes that come pre-loaded in the software, on topics like state capitals or trivia questions about animals. You might even find you learn a few things while you're using Alexa to relieve your boredom. Other simple games that Alexa plays include Rock, Paper, Scissors and Tic Tac Toe.

If you've got more time on your hands, check out The Magic Door, a speech command-based choose your own adventure game with a variety of different stories to choose from.

Easter Eggs are things Alexa can say that are not formally documented anywhere. They are cute and funny phrases that various Alexa users have found. Alexa possesses hundreds of Easter Eggs within her always growing brain. These amusing hidden phrases are triggered by asking just the right questions. The list of some of Alexa's Easter Eggs below has been compiled from LinkedIn.

The Easter Eggs are as follows:

1. Alexa, 70 factorial

2. Alexa, all grown-ups were once children...

3. Alexa, all your base belongs to us.

4. Alexa, All's well that ends well

5. Alexa, Am I hot?

6. Alexa, Are there UFOs?

7. Alexa, Are we alone in the universe?

8. Alexa, Are we in the Matrix?

9. Alexa, Are you a robot?

10. Alexa, Are you alive?

11. Alexa, are you connected to the Internet?

12. Alexa, Are you crazy?

13. Alexa, Are you female?

14. Alexa, Are you happy?

15. Alexa, Are you horny?

16. Alexa, Are you in love?

17. Alexa, are you lying?

18. Alexa, Are you my mommy?

19. Alexa, Are you okay?

20. Alexa, Are you real? (multiple)

21. Alexa, are you single?

22. Alexa, are you sky net?

23. Alexa, Are you smart?

24. Alexa, Are you stupid?

25. Alexa, Aren't you a little short for a Stormtrooper?

26. Alexa, beam me up.

27. Alexa, can I ask a question?

28. Alexa, can you give me some money? (ask twice)

29. Alexa, can you lie?

30. Alexa, can you pass the Turing test?

31. Alexa, can you smell that?

32. Alexa, Cheers!

33. Alexa, Daisy Daisy.

34. Alexa, define rock paper scissors lizard spock

35. Alexa, define supercalifragilisticexpialodocious.

36. Alexa, did you fart?

37. Alexa, did you get my email?

38. Alexa, Do a barrel

Conclusion

Amazon designed Alexa so that each user's experience with the program could be completely customized to their needs. The expansion of their device catalogue with the new Look and Show only adds to your options, and almost anything you want to do with Alexa can be accomplished by enabling a Skill or using IFTTT.

The information included in this book is a basic overview of what you can do with Alexa, enough to get you started with using the device, but the truth is that Alexa is constantly evolving—one of the things that makes it so incredibly valuable. New Skills are constantly being added to expand Alexa's functionality. Since the program is completely Cloud-based, it is instantly updated and always being improved, often in direct response to consumer demands.

Being able to adjust your lights or heat with your voice used to be the stuff of science fiction. Even once it became possible, it was the exclusive domain of the wealthy, who could afford to set up elaborate smart home systems that had to be installed by professionals. This has changed again, however, and if you buy a $30 Echo Dot and a few smart plugs, you can set up a smart home for less than $200. Realizing just how affordable it can be is often enough to make skeptics want to try it.

Now that you've gotten the basics of your device, don't be afraid to explore more options. The more popular Alexa becomes, the more companies are jumping on the bandwagon with their own smart versions of devices (and associated Alexa Skills). Even if you only use its basic on-board capabilities, getting familiar with Alexa will save you time and headaches, helping you to keep your life organized so that you can focus on the things you want to be doing.

I hope that you really enjoyed reading my book. If you want to help me to produce more materials like this, then **please leave a positive review on Amazon.**

Thanks for buying the book anyway!

I think next books will also be interesting for you:

Amazon Customer Service

Alexa: Get The Best Out Of Your Personal Assistant

<u>Amazon Prime and Kindle Lending Library</u>

Made in the USA
Middletown, DE
05 December 2017